Maximum Strength Expungement

How to File and Win Michigan Expungements

DEDICATION

To my kids who make each day amazing

CONTENTS

INTRODUCTION

This book is quite simple. You have a criminal record, and you're wondering if you can get rid of that record. Many clients hire me, and pay me a lot of money to work on their expungement case with fantastic results. That's just one approach; the law doesn't require a client to have a lawyer for their expungement filing, but it's a complicated process, and that makes people very nervous.

The purpose of this book is not to be a substitute for hiring an attorney, but rather an educational tool to better inform the general public about the process, and a number of thoughts on how to best approach this legal problem.

Each reader will decide if they wish to try the process on their own, or to hire an attorney. The more information available in making that decision, the better informed that decision will ultimately be for the reader.

This book is not meant to be legal advice, it's a mere education tool to help the public better understand the process. You should reach out to me directly to discuss your case before adopting any legal strategy that may be mentioned in this book.

This book is meant to be an easy read, and quite casual. I wanted to write something that sounds more like a conversation in my office rather than a legal research book.

Attorney | Jonathan Paul

Jonathan's practice focuses exclusively on criminal law, representing doctors, nurses attorneys, executives, senior military officers, teachers, professional and college athletes, pilots, and the hard working people of Michigan who find themselves charged with a crime. Jonathan has authored numerous books on Michigan criminal defense.

Jonathan has been recognized by Super Lawyers Magazine as a "Rising Star" the past five years (2013, 2014, 2015, 2016 & 2017); the prestigious magazine selects the top 2.5 percent of attorneys in Michigan. Jonathan's selection by Super Lawyers Magazine was featured in Hour Detroit Magazine and the New York Times.

Jonathan's work has earned him a "Superb" 10.0 AVVO Rating by his peers and clients.

Jonathan is licensed to practice law in the State of Michigan and New York. Jonathan graduated from the University of Michigan Law School, and is a former New York City Assistant District Attorney and former Oakland County (Michigan) Assistant Prosecutor.

Jonathan prosecuted thousands of high profile felony, misdemeanor and drunk driving cases. During his career as a prosecutor, Jonathan had a 100% conviction rate, having never lost a jury or bench trial. Along with being a former prosecutor, Jonathan was also a faculty member at Kingsborough College in New York City, where he lectured on criminal law, criminal justice and constitutional law.

Jonathan resides in Ann Arbor with his wife and two children, and is a life-long fan of the New York Yankees, and everything University of Michigan.

THE PROCESS

DO YOU QUALIFY?

I receive hundreds of phone calls and emails a year from prospective expungement clients. The client usually leaves a voicemail or in their email provides limited information about their case. When I reach back out to them, I ask them a number of key questions.

1. What charge would you like to expunge?
2. In what court were you convicted?
3. What was the date of your sentencing?
4. Were you placed on probation, or did you go to jail or prison?
5. What if any other cases have you had in the past?
6. What if any charges have you had in the past that were dismissed?

It's possible that the client is not quite sure about some of these answers, but I ask them to do their best to figure them out, because it's the difference between being eligible or not-eligible to have your record expunged in Michigan.

I ask the charge, because some charges in Michigan are not eligible for expungement, most notable charges found in the Motor Vehicle Code. I ask the court, because it tells me if it's a felony or misdemeanor, and for my own practice purposes, if it's something I would take on geographically. I ask the date, because there are "waiting periods" before a record can be expunged in Michigan. I ask about probation and jail/prison, because the clock starts when those come to an end, not the sentencing date.

I ask about prior cases, because there is a limit on having your record expunged based upon your prior criminal record, and cases that have already been dismissed against you will count as charges as if they were not dismissed.

If the client is not sure of these answers, I advise them to run their criminal history online, which I will discuss in more detail, or to contact the courts where they had their criminal case. The client won't be able to access non-public dismissals online, but may be able to retrieve those court records with photo identification in person.

Here are a number of items to keep in mind when determining eligibility:

If you have a felony with the maximum punishment being life in prison, you are not eligible. A violation or attempted violation of a criminal sexual conduct offense and most child abuse offenses are not eligible (see specific degrees for specific answer)

Any misdemeanor or felony found in the Motor Vehicle Code (MCL 257.1 etc) such as drunk driving, reckless driving, fleeing and eluding, DWLS are not eligible for expungement.

A felony conviction for domestic violence with previous misdemeanor convictions is not eligible. The same holds true for human trafficking and terrorism offenses.

Assuming one of those apply, we then move onto the number of convictions. Starting in 2015, the number of prior convictions became more forgiving in terms of overall number.

The current expungement statute permits a person convicted of not more than one felony and not more than two misdemeanors to petition the convicting court to set aside the felony under MCL 780.621(1)(a).

So this means if you have two or more felony convictions, you are not eligible, and if you have three or more misdemeanor convictions, you are not eligible. This isn't to say you won't be eligible sometime in the future as the law has expanded in past years, and it could continue to expand in the future.

When counting your past convictions, the law will consider deferred convictions as actual convictions for eligibility purposes. Dismissals under the following are considered convictions:

- MCL 436.1703 (purchase, consumption, or possession of alcoholic liquor by minor)
- MCL 600.1070 (admission into drug treatment court) and 600.1209 (veterans treatment court)
- MCL 762.13 (assignment as youthful trainee under the Holmes Youthful Trainee Act) or 769.4a(domestic violence)
- MCL 333.7411 (controlled substances)
- MCL 750.350a (taking or retaining child by adoptive or natural parent) or 750.430 (licensed health care professional engaging in practice with unlawful bodily alcohol content of .05 or more or under the influence of a controlled substance)
- any other Michigan state or local law similar in nature and applicability to those listed above that provides for the deferral and dismissal of

a felony or misdemeanor charge <u>MCL 780.621(2)</u>.

This means if you had an MIP case when you were 20, which was dismissed under a referral program, a drug possession case when you were 24, which was dismissed and a retail fraud case on your public record, you would have three convictions for purposes of expungement, and not be eligible.

The court may also use past expunged convictions against the person seeking expungement. Assuming you're still within the limits number wise, you would then move on to the timing of your prior convictions.

The question now becomes, has it been at least five years since any of the following events:

- imposition of the sentence for the conviction that the person seeks to set aside
- completion of probation imposed for the conviction that the applicant seeks to set aside
- discharge from parole imposed for the conviction that the applicant seeks to set aside
- completion of any term of imprisonment imposed for the conviction that the applicant seeks to set aside

If you're still eligible based upon the prior questions, the final determination will be if there are any pending criminal charges against you.

Even if the answer to that final question is NO, it doesn't mean your criminal record reflects the same. I've had clients ticketed, arrested or investigated many years ago, and they ended up never being charged or even going to court, but their Michigan State Police record indicates a "pending" or "open" case from 15-20 years ago.

In reality, nothing ended up happening, but MSP doesn't actively pull records and close out cases. I've had to correct client's criminal records prior to filing for expungement in order to avoid this final step that could disqualify your application.

Unsure about your record, you can order your Michigan criminal history from the Michigan State Police by googling Internet Criminal History Access Tool or ICHAT Michigan.

EXPUNGEMENT A TO Z

Now that we've determined that you're eligible, it's time to discuss how to get from pen to paper to the judge signing an order to expunge for your record.

Step one is to acquire the proper forms. These forms are available online. Google "SCAO form MC 227 (Application to Set Aside Conviction) and SCAO MC 228 (Order on Application to Set Aside Conviction)

Step two is to contact the district or circuit court where the conviction occurred and order the certified copy of the conviction record. The older the case the more difficult it may be to obtain the record. This could be the case for a place like Frank Murphy in Detroit, as many of the files are not computerized and stored in a warehouse.

It's probably wise to go in-person and put a name to a face in ordering these records. You may need to follow-up multiple times to get these records. Be respectful of the staff and don't get frustrated; it's not the clerks fault that the system may not be efficient.

The record of these convictions must be certified meaning that the clerk has added a level of certification either with a special stamp, signature or seal. The record might be a judgment of sentence, a probation discharge, register of actions or all of the above. It's always wise to get more paperwork than less paperwork as you will need the information on these forms to fill out your application, and to include in your application for expungement.

You're looking for information about the charge, the court, exact date of conviction, date of sentence and what the sentence was on the case. Be sure to have five copies of these records for the process. Again, make sure it is certified.

The next step is to obtain fingerprints with your local police agency. It does not need to be the same police agency from your case, and it doesn't even need to be a police agency in Michigan. Many people live outside of Michigan seek expungement, and can go to their own local agency.

You may be able to walk-in to do the prints if the agency is not busy, or call ahead and schedule an appointment. There may be a small fee involved, and you must use the RI-8 fingerprint form, which must be filled out.

Once you have all the relevant information, it's time to work on your application. You will need five copies and the application must be signed under oath with a notary public or a court clerk.

Once you have five signed applications, it's time to go visit the court clerk at the courthouse where you're seeking expungement. You must bring the original signed and notarized application, the original certified copy of the prior conviction, which you seek to expunge, and five copies of both the application and the certified record.

The clerk at the courthouse will provide you a hearing date with the original judge on your case if they are still on the bench, or the new judge, which followed is succession of the prior judge.

The clerk will hand back the five copies with the hearing date filled out under the "notice of hearing" section on the application. This date will typically be 90-120 days in the future as the Michigan State Police will need time to respond to the application to verify your criminal history.

The Michigan State Police (MSP) has requested that hearings be set at least 90–120 days from filing to ensure that they will have time to respond to the application.

Ok, you're back in your car, and you're leaving the courthouse will all of these papers, what do you do now?

It's time to provide notice of the hearing and notice of your application to the other required parties in the case. Just because you're eligible under the law, doesn't mean the judge will sign the order. The law allows, and requires all other interested parties to have a say in the expungement. Here is a breakdown of who must be notified, and how to provide the proper notice.

First up, the Michigan State Police must receive a copy of the application, a copy of the certified record of conviction, the fingerprint card (RI-8) and $50 fee payable to the State of Michigan. The mailing address for MSP is the following:

P.O. Box 30634
Lansing, Michigan 48909

Best to verify that mailing address by calling the Michigan State Police at 517-241-0606.

Next, you must send the Michigan Attorney General a copy of the application and a copy of the certified record of conviction. The mailing address for Attorney General is the following:

Michigan Department of Attorney General
Corrections Division
P.O. Box 30217
Lansing, MI 48909

Next, you must provide the copy of the application and the copy of the certified record of conviction to the prosecuting attorney. This information should be listed on the certified record of conviction. Do not assume that it's the County prosecutor, as most cases are actually prosecuted by villages, townships and cities rather than the county.

The best resource for the mailing address for the prosecutor is Google. All prosecutor information should be available online including the name of the prosecutor, mailing address and phone number. If you're not computer savvy, ask the court clerk to provide you this information; do it with a smile, and they will help you.

With your final two copies of the application, you must fill out the section at the bottom called "proof of service. Retain one copy and provide the court the other copy, which informs the court that you served the Michigan State Police, Michigan Attorney General and the prosecuting attorney with your application, certified copy of conviction, and for the MSP, the $50 fee along with the fingerprint card.

Next, take the MC 228 form and fill out the heading, and leave the majority of the order to be completed by the judge. Many courts are going with e-filing, but always best to bring four copies with you to court in case the judge asks for them.

You have all your mailings out, your orders ready, and now you need to wait 3 to 4 months to go to court. During this time, Michigan State Police will verify your criminal record using your fingerprints and send a response to the court. The Michigan Attorney General and the prosecuting attorney will review your application and respond.

They will either file a response asking the court to NOT expunge your record for the following reasons, or simply take no position and leave the decision to the discretion of the court. Rarely if ever will they agree that the record should be expunged, but the "discretion of the court" response is what you're looking for in the response.

If the MSP verifies your public and non-public record and agrees you're eligible, and the prosecutors leave the decision to the discretion of the court, you're in a strong position to have the judge sign your order.

On the date of your hearing, you should show-up early, and check in with the clerk of the court. Go to the correct courtroom, let the judge's staff know you are present. They may suggest you check-in with the prosecutor, or may just tell you to be patient and your case will be called.

Once the case is called, the judge will address your request and may simply sign the order or engage in a conversation with you. A judge has typically made up his/her mind already, but may want to learn something more about your background, motivations and future plans.

It's always best to be humble about the process as expungement is a privilege, it is not a right. The judge is making the decision of expungement in the context of the best interest of society, not in the best interest of your life.

If expungement is granted, thank the judge for his/her time, and ask the clerk whether or not the court clerk will send the copies of the order to the

Michigan State Police Central Records Division. It's always a best practice to send a copy of the order to the Michigan Attorney General and the prosecuting attorney as well.

It's best practice to wait a few weeks before re-running your ICHAT online to verify the record has been expunged. If not, don't worry, the process takes some time, and you might want to follow-up with the court clerk to verify when the order was mailed out.

If the expungement request is NOT granted, a subsequent filing cannot be filed for three years after the date of the decision. The court can set an earlier date in their ruling. If the judge is not prepared to expunge, they may provide you a reason, and it may be something you can address in the near future, and it's best to request a time to come back prior to the typical three year waiting period.

This A to Z process should be sufficient for most expungement applications in most courts with most judges, but what I have laid out is only the barebones of expungement. It's like applying for a job by emailing or mailing your resume with nothing else provided to the recipient.

Sure you might get the job, and the judge might sign your order, but there is a lot more to do in order to improve your changes of the Michigan Attorney General and prosecuting attorney keeping their swords at home, and leaving the decision to the judge, and to convince the judge to expunge your record.

The following chapter discusses some techniques and extra information that my clients provide to the Michigan State Police, the Michigan Attorney General, the prosecuting attorney and the presiding judge.

The following insight is not meant to be legal advice, and it's best to consult an attorney prior to handling this on your own, but the law does not require an attorney, and the purpose of this entire book is to educate the reader, and help you make the right decision for your own situation.

HOW TO WIN YOUR EXPUNGEMENT

The prior chapter provided you the nuts and bolts on starting the expungement process to getting your request in front of the judge, and simply hoping for the best in court. With or without an attorney, there is a lot more that can be done to improve your chances of having your request approved.

When I work with a new client on expungement, I put myself in the position of the police, prosecutor and the judge. I imagine sitting at my desk and the client's expungement application arrives in the mail.

I open the letter and review the request; everything looks in order, and the person followed the rule. Looks like the person is eligible under the law, but is that really enough?

Depending upon the charge and when it happened, this is either a relatively easy decision or something that I may want more information on.

As the Michigan State Police, I am simply confirming eligibly, but as the Michigan Attorney General and prosecuting attorney, I am looking at a valid conviction from years ago where a prosecutor, the police, a judge, probation and possibly victims and witnesses were involved. Does time alone mean this incident should be cleared from the public eyes?

The goal with the Michigan Attorney General and prosecuting attorney is for them to take no position. If the Attorney General takes no position, they will not show up for the expungement hearing. The prosecuting will be present, and will have the opportunity to say something in court about your request.

Ideally you want the prosecuting attorney to leave the decision to the discretion of the court. It's a lot easier to get a judge to sign an order which clears your record when the person who prosecuted you is not taking any position and not contesting the request.

Any victim involved in the case would have an opportunity to speak in court either directly or via the prosecuting attorney. If no victim existed then it's not a factor, but if there was a victim, the ideal situation is they have nothing to add to the proceeding.

It's my approach that no matter the charge(s), timeline, court or judge, it's always good to provide more information about my client.

I like to go back to when the office happened, and layout in great detail what my client has done since the original conviction. The more time that has gone by, the better argument to made that the client is a new person, and has grown and learned from their past.

The client may have graduated from high school, college, obtained graduate or technical degrees. The client may have advanced in their careers, taken on more responsibility in the workforce.

Maybe the client has been married, had children, moved away, and are living a whole new life since this incident.

I ask all of my clients to provide me all the details of their life since the prior conviction. This might mean a resume, proof of education, letters of reference from their career, family or school.

Sometimes the conviction stemmed from a substance abuse or psychological issue, which it would be important to show continued treatment and progress with counseling, rehab, support group meetings.

I always ask my client what their original sentence as for their case, and if they aren't sure, it is usually listed in the discharge from probation or the judgement of sentence.

I will usually encourage my client that as part of our application that we do additional community service. It may seem odd to do community service ten years after the incident, but the standard for the judge in making their decision is whether it is in the best interest of society to expunge the record.

We want to do everything in our power to show that our request is in the best interest, because my client is a positive person in the community, and erasing their public record will allow the client to get further engaged in positive aspects of the community, which the criminal record may be interfering with at the time of application.

It's always beneficial if we can point to a specific example as to how the conviction has impacted my client's life. The reason can be as obvious as lost opportunity in the workforce to not being able to pass a background check for your kid's field trip.

When I work with a client, we follow all the steps outlined in the previous chapter. The client simply gets their own fingerprints, and I do everything else.

From acquiring the documents from the court, to communicating with the court on the hearing date, to mailing out all of the copies to the Michigan State Police, Michigan Attorney General and the prosecuting attorney.

Along with the standard application, I file a Motion to Set Aside Conviction with all parties including the court. The motion gives a roadmap to the reader in the same way that a great cover letter can make a resume come alive for applying for a job.

This motion lays out everything about the prior conviction which we seek to expunge in great detail. We're acknowledging the past, embracing the sentence, which was successfully completed.

If this is the only offense which my client has on their record, we can emphasize that for the reader that this was an isolated moment in time, providing more context about my client's age, and situation at the time, and pivot to the client remaining out of trouble since this incident occurred.

This is where we lay out the "what have you been

up to lately" answer to the judge's natural inclination to be curious about recent events.

We lay out in great detail how the client has lived their life since this incident, and we provide exhibits and attachments for the reader.

We then go step by step over the eligibility factors and tell the reader why the client is eligible, which is backed up by the Michigan State Police response.

We then focus on the best interest of the public welfare analysis acknowledging that this process is a privilege and not a right; always best to be humble and properly understand the weight of the decision that must be made by the judge.

Along with this comprehensive approach to the expungement process, you may prefer to go to court with an experienced attorney who can simply say, "ok go sit right over there, I will take care of everything".

As an attorney on an expungement case, I would confirm that all parties have been served, I would receive and review their responses and discuss them with my client. If there is a timing issue or someone was not served, we would fix it, and re-schedule the hearing date.

If we're good to go for court, I check-in with the prosecutor, confirm that they are not taking a position, and if they are, to help better understand why, and potentially address their concerns.

Once the case is called, I walk up to the podium with my client with the confidence that the judge has a full picture of who my client is outside of the charge, the year, and "please expunge" request. I want the judge to view my client in two contexts; where the client was when this happened, and where they are now in life.

It's my goal that judge is impressed with how my client has since reacted to their past, and how they have grown as a member of society. I want the judge to tell my client that they are proud of them, and it's their privilege to expunge the record, because the client has earned that result. We never go to court assuming or hoping for the best; we go in with a plan, and we're confident that the proper steps have been followed, and we're presenting a request that makes sense to the judge.

MICHIGAN TRIAL COURT DIRECTORY

WAYNE COUNTY

3rd Circuit Court

Coleman A. Young Municipal Center

2 Woodward Avenue

Detroit, MI 48226

(313) 224-5261

Honorable Robert J. Colombo, Jr., Chief Judge

Honorable David J. Allen, Circuit Judge

Honorable Mariam Bazzi, Circuit Judge

Honorable Annette J. Berry, Circuit Judge

Honorable Gregory D. Bill, Circuit Judge

Honorable Ulysses W. Boykin, Circuit Judge

Honorable Karen Y. Braxton, Circuit Judge

Honorable Megan Maher Brennan, Circuit Judge

Ms. Zenell Brown, Court Administrator

Honorable Thomas Cameron, Circuit Judge

Honorable Jerome C. Cavanagh, Circuit Judge

Honorable Eric William Cholack, Circuit Judge

Honorable James R. Chylinski, Circuit Judge

Honorable Kevin J. Cox, Circuit Judge

Honorable Melissa Anne Cox, Circuit Judge

Honorable Paul John Cusick, Circuit Judge

Honorable Christopher D. Dingell, Circuit Judge

Honorable Charlene M. Elder, Circuit Judge

Honorable Vonda R. Evans, Circuit Judge

Honorable Wanda Evans, Circuit Judge

Honorable Edward Ewell, Jr., Circuit Judge

Honorable Patricia Susan Fresard, Circuit Judge

Honorable Sheila Ann Gibson, Circuit Judge

Honorable John H. Gillis, Jr., Circuit Judge

Honorable Alexis Glendening, Circuit Judge

Honorable David Alan Groner, Circuit Judge

Honorable Richard B. Halloran, Circuit Judge

Honorable Adel A. Harb, Circuit Judge

Honorable Cynthia Gray Hathaway, Circuit Judge

Honorable Dana Margaret Hathaway, Circuit Judge

Honorable Daniel Arthur Hathaway, Circuit Judge

Honorable Thomas M. J. Hathaway, Circuit Judge

Honorable Charles S. Hegarty, Circuit Judge

Honorable Catherine Heise, Circuit Judge

Honorable Susan L. Hubbard, Circuit Judge

Honorable Muriel D. Hughes, Circuit Judge

Honorable Edward Joseph, Circuit Judge

Honorable Connie Marie Kelley, Circuit Judge

Honorable Timothy Michael Kenny, Circuit Judge

Honorable Qiana D. Lillard, Circuit Judge

Honorable Kathleen M. McCarthy, Circuit Judge

Honorable Bruce U. Morrow, Circuit Judge

Honorable John A. Murphy, Circuit Judge

Honorable Lynne A. Pierce, Circuit Judge

Honorable Lita Masini Popke, Circuit Judge

Honorable Kelly Ramsey, Circuit Judge

Honorable Richard M. Skutt, Circuit Judge

Honorable Mark T. Slavens, Circuit Judge

Honorable Leslie Kim Smith, Circuit Judge

Honorable Virgil C. Smith, Circuit Judge

Honorable Martha M. Snow, Circuit Judge

Honorable Craig S. Strong, Circuit Judge

Honorable Brian R. Sullivan, Circuit Judge

Honorable Lawrence S. Talon, Circuit Judge

Honorable Deborah A. Thomas, Circuit Judge

Honorable Margaret M. Van Houten, Circuit Judge

Honorable Shannon N. Walker, Circuit Judge

16th District Court (Livonia)

32765 Five Mile Rd.

Livonia, MI 48154

(734) 466-2500

Honorable Sean P. Kavanagh, Chief Judge

Honorable Kathleen J. McCann, District Judge

Ms. Natalie Stojcevska, Court Administrator

17th District Court (Redford)

15111 Beech-Daly Rd.

Redford, MI 48239

(313) 387-2790

Honorable Karen Khalil, Chief Judge

Mr. Matthew Sawicki, Court Administrator

Honorable Charlotte L. Wirth, District Judge

18th District Court (Westland)

36675 Ford Rd.

Westland, MI 48185

(734) 595-8720

Honorable Sandra A. Cicirelli, Chief Judge

Mr. James Gibbs, Court Administrator

Honorable Mark A. McConnell, District Judge

19th District Court (Dearborn)

16077 Michigan Ave.

Dearborn, MI 48126

(313) 943-2060

Honorable Sam A. Salamey, Chief Judge

Mr. Eric F. Cyman, Court Administrator

Honorable L. Eugene Hunt, Jr., District Judge

Honorable Mark W. Somers, District Judge

20th District Court (Dearborn Heights)

25637 Michigan Ave.

Dearborn Heights, MI 48125

(313) 277-7480

Honorable Mark J. Plawecki, Chief Judge

Ms. Michelle Adkins, Court Administrator

Honorable David Turfe, District Judge

21st District Court (Garden City)

6000 N. Middlebelt Rd.

Garden City, MI 48135

(734) 793-1680

Honorable Richard L. Hammer, Jr., Chief Judge

Ms. Kristin Remer, Court Administrator

22nd District Court (Inkster)

26279 Michigan Ave.

Inkster, MI 48141

(313) 277-8200

Honorable Sabrina L. Johnson, Chief Judge

Ms. Priscilla Gibbs, Court Administrator

23rd District Court (Taylor)

23365 Goddard

Taylor, MI 48180

(734) 374-1334

Honorable Geno Salomone, Chief Judge

Honorable Joseph D. Slaven, District Judge

Ms. Deanna Warunek, Court Administrator

24th District Court (Allen Park)

6515 Roosevelt Rd.

Allen Park, MI 48101

(313) 928-0535

Honorable John T. Courtright, Chief Judge

Ms. Dawn Grubbs, Court Administrator

Honorable Richard A. Page, District Judge

25th District Court (Lincoln Park)

1475 Cleophus

Lincoln Park, MI 48146

(313) 382-8603

Honorable Gregory A. Clifton, Chief Judge

Ms. Teri Michael, Court Administrator

Honorable David J. Zelenak, District Judge

27th District Court (Wyandotte)

2015 Biddle Ave.

Wyandotte, MI 48192

(734) 324-4475

Honorable Randy L. Kalmbach, Chief Judge

Ms. Stacie Nevalo, Court Administrator

28th District Court (Southgate)

14720 Reaume Parkway

Southgate, MI 48195

(734) 258-3068

Honorable James A. Kandrevas, Chief Judge

Mr. Jeffrey W. Meussner, Court Administrator

29th District Court (Wayne)

34808 Sims Ave.

Wayne, MI 48184

(734) 722-5220

Honorable Laura Redmond Mack, Chief Judge

Ms. Linda Gable, Court Administrator

30th District Court (Highland Park)

12050 Woodward Ave.

Highland Park, MI 48203

(313) 252-0300

Honorable Brigette R. Officer-Hill, Chief Judge

Ms. Robynn M. Diamond, Court Administrator

31st District Court (Hamtramck)

3401 Evaline Ave.

Hamtramck, MI 48212

(313) 800-5248

Honorable Alexis G Krot, Chief Judge

Mr. Benjamin Ruby, Court Administrator

32A District Court (Harper Woods)

19617 Harper Ave.

Harper Woods, MI 48225

(313) 343-2590

Honorable Daniel S. Palmer, Chief Judge

Ms. Marcy Ruggirello, Court Administrator

33rd District Court (Woodhaven)

19000 Van Horn

Woodhaven, MI 48183

(734) 671-0201

Honorable Jennifer Coleman Hesson, Chief Judge

Honorable James Kurt Kersten, District Judge

Honorable Michael K. McNally, District Judge

Ms. Amy Zawacki, Court Administrator

34th District Court (Romulus)

11131 Wayne Rd.

Romulus, MI 48174

(734) 941-4462

Honorable Tina Brooks Green, Chief Judge

Mr. Alan Hindman, Court Administrator

Honorable Brian A. Oakley, District Judge

Honorable David M. Parrott, District Judge

35th District Court (Plymouth)

660 Plymouth Rd.

Plymouth, MI 48170

(734) 459-4740

Magistrate Frank Whren

Honorable Michael J. Gerou, Chief Judge

Ms. Pam Avdoulos, Court Administrator

Honorable Ronald W. Lowe, District Judge

Honorable James A. Plakas, District Judge

36th District Court (Detroit)

421 Madison Ave.

Detroit, MI 48226

(313) 965-2200

Honorable Nancy McCaughan Blount, Chief Judge

Honorable Lydia Nance Adams, District Judge

Honorable Roberta C. Archer, District Judge

Honorable Christopher Michael Blount, District Judge

Honorable Izetta F. Bright, District Judge

Honorable Demetria Brue, District Judge

Honorable Esther Lynise Bryant-Weekes, District Judge

Honorable Donald Coleman, District Judge

Honorable Kahlilia Yvette Davis, District Judge

Honorable Prentis Edwards, Jr., District Judge

Honorable Deborah Geraldine Ford, District Judge

Honorable Austin William Garrett, District Judge

Honorable Ruth Ann Garrett, District Judge

Honorable Ronald Giles, District Judge

Honorable Adrienne Hinnant-Johnson, District Judge

Honorable Shannon A. Holmes, District Judge

Honorable Patricia L. Jefferson, District Judge

Honorable Kenyetta Stanford Jones, District Judge

Honorable Alicia A. Jones-Coleman, District Judge

Honorable Kenneth J. King, District Judge

Honorable Deborah L. Langston, District Judge

Honorable William McConico, District Judge

Honorable Donna R. Milhouse, District Judge

Honorable B. Pennie Millender, District Judge

Honorable Cylenthia LaToye Miller, District Judge

Ms. Kelli Moore Owen, Court Administrator

Honorable David Perkins, District Judge

Honorable Kevin F. Robbins, District Judge

Honorable David S. Robinson, Jr., District Judge

Honorable Michael E. Wagner, District Judge

Honorable Larry D. Williams, Jr., District Judge

Grosse Pte. Municipal Court (Grosse Pointe City)

17147 Maumee

Grosse Pointe, MI 48230

(313) 343-5262

Honorable Russell F. Ethridge, Chief Judge

Ms. Kim Silvestro, Court Administrator

Grosse Pte. Farms Municipal Court (Grosse Pointe Farms)

90 Kerby Rd.

Grosse Pte. Farms, MI 48236

(313) 885-2104

Honorable Matthew R. Rumora, Chief Judge

Ms. Madeline Eberhardt, Court Administrator

Grosse Pte. Park Municipal Court

15115 E. Jefferson Ave.

Grosse Pte. Park, MI 48230

(313) 822-3535

Honorable Carl F. Jarboe, Chief Judge

Ms. Susan Thomas, Court Administrator

Grosse Pte. Woods Municipal Court (Grosse Pointe Woods)

20025 Mack Plaza Drive

Grosse Pte. Woods, MI 48236

(313) 343-2455

Honorable Theodore A. Metry, Chief Judge

Ms. Susan Tobin, Court Administrator

OAKLAND COUNTY

6th Circuit Court

Courthouse Tower

1200 N. Telegraph Rd.

Pontiac, MI 48341

(248) 858-0345

Honorable Nanci J. Grant, Chief Judge

Honorable James M. Alexander, Circuit Judge

Honorable Martha Anderson, Circuit Judge

Honorable Leo Bowman, Circuit Judge

Honorable Mary Ellen Brennan, Circuit Judge

Honorable Rae Lee Chabot, Circuit Judge

Honorable Lisa Ortlieb Gorcyca, Circuit Judge

Honorable Hala Y. Jarbou, Circuit Judge

Honorable Shalina D. Kumar, Circuit Judge

Honorable Denise Langford-Morris, Circuit Judge

Honorable Lisa Langton, Circuit Judge

Honorable Jeffery S. Matis, Circuit Judge

Honorable Cheryl A. Matthews, Circuit Judge

Honorable Karen D. McDonald, Circuit Judge

Honorable Phyllis C. McMillen, Circuit Judge

Honorable Daniel Patrick O'Brien, Circuit Judge

Honorable Wendy Lynn Potts, Circuit Judge

Honorable Victoria Ann Valentine, Circuit Judge

Honorable Michael D. Warren, Jr., Circuit Judge

Mr. Kevin Oeffner, Court Administrator

43rd District Court (Hazel Park)

43 E. Nine Mile Rd.

Hazel Park, MI 48030

(248) 547-3034

Honorable Joseph Longo, Chief Judge

Honorable Charles G. Goedert, District Judge

Honorable Keith P. Hunt, District Judge

Ms. Diana M. Nimmoor, Court Administrator

43rd District Court (Ferndale)

305 E. Nine Mile Rd.

Ferndale, MI 48220

(248) 547-8700

Honorable Joseph Longo, Chief Judge

Honorable Charles G. Goedert, District Judge

Honorable Keith P. Hunt, District Judge

Ms. Linda S. Carroll, Court Administrator

43rd District Court (Madison Heights)

200 W. Thirteen Mile Rd.

Madison Heights, MI 48071

(248) 583-1800

Honorable Joseph Longo, Chief Judge

Honorable Charles G. Goedert, District Judge

Honorable Keith P. Hunt, District Judge

Ms. Sharon L. Arseneault, Court Administrator

44th District Court (Royal Oak)

PO Box 20

400 E. 11 Mile Road

Royal Oak, MI 48068

(248) 246-3600

Honorable Derek W. Meinecke, Chief Judge

Honorable James L. Wittenberg, District Judge

Mr. Gary W. Dodge, Court Administrator

45th District Court (Oak Park)

13600 Oak Park Blvd.

Oak Park, MI 48237

(248) 691-7433

Honorable Michelle Friedman Appel, Chief Judge

Honorable David M. Gubow, District Judge

Ms. Nancy Waldmann, Court Administrator

46th District Court (Southfield)

PO Box 2055

26000 Evergreen Rd.

Southfield, MI 48076

(248) 796-5800

Honorable Shelia R. Johnson, Chief Judge

Honorable Cynthia Arvant, District Judge

Honorable Debra Nance, District Judge

Ms. Renee R. Shelide, Court Administrator

47th District Court (Farmington Hills)

31605 W. Eleven Mile Road

Farmington Hills, MI 48336

(248) 871-2900

Honorable James Brady, Chief Judge

Honorable Marla E. Parker, District Judge

Mr. David L. Walsh, Court Administrator

48th District Court (Bloomfield Hills)

PO Box 3200

4280 Telegraph Rd.

Bloomfield Hills, MI 48302

(248) 647-1141

Honorable Marc Barron, Chief Judge

Honorable Diane D'Agostini, District Judge

Honorable Kimberly Small, District Judge

Mr. Jim VerPloeg, Court Administrator

50th District Court (Pontiac)

70 N. Saginaw

Pontiac, MI 48342

(248) 758-3800

Honorable Cynthia Thomas Walker, Chief Judge

Honorable Ronda Fowlkes Gross, District Judge

Honorable Michael C. Martinez, District Judge

Honorable Preston G. Thomas, District Judge

Ms. Lynette Ward, Court Administrator

51st District Court (Waterford)

5100 Civic Center Drive

Waterford, MI 48329

(248) 674-4655

Honorable Richard D. Kuhn, Jr., Chief Judge

Honorable Todd A. Fox, District Judge

Ms. Jennifer Thom, Court Administrator

52nd District Court – (Novi)

48150 Grand River Ave.

Novi, MI 48374

(248) 305-6080

Honorable Julie A. Nicholson, Chief Judge

Honorable Robert Bondy, District Judge

Honorable Thomas David Law, District Judge

Honorable Travis Reeds, District Judge

Ms. Alexandra Black, Court Administrator

52nd District Court (Clarkston)

5850 Lorac

Clarkston, MI 48346

(248) 625-4888

Honorable Julie A. Nicholson, Chief Judge

Honorable Joseph G. Fabrizio, District Judge

Honorable Kelley Renae Kostin, District Judge

Ms. Sharon Rupe, Court Administrator

52nd District Court (Rochester Hills)

700 Barclay Circle

Rochester Hills, MI 48307

(248) 853-5553

Honorable Julie A. Nicholson, Chief Judge

Honorable Lisa L. Asadoorian, District Judge

Honorable Nancy Tolwin Carniak, District Judge

Mr. Brian Matthew Henderson, Court Administrator

52nd District Court (Troy)

520 W. Big Beaver Road

Troy, MI 48084

(248) 528-0400

Honorable Julie A. Nicholson, Chief Judge

Honorable Kirsten Nielsen Hartig, District Judge

Honorable Maureen M. McGinnis, District Judge

Ms. B. Jill Palulian, Court Administrator

MACOMB COUNTY

16th Circuit Court (Macomb)

Macomb County Court Building

40 N. Main

Mt. Clemens, MI 48043

(586) 469-5150

Honorable James M. Biernat, Jr., Chief Judge

Ms. Julie Bovenschen, Court Administrator

Honorable Richard L. Caretti, Circuit Judge

Honorable Diane M. Druzinski, Circuit Judge

Honorable Jennifer Faunce, Circuit Judge

Honorable James M. Maceroni, Circuit Judge

Honorable Carl J. Marlinga, Circuit Judge

Honorable Racheal Rancilio, Circuit Judge

Honorable Edward A. Servitto, Jr., Circuit Judge

Honorable Michael E. Servitto, Circuit Judge

Honorable Mark S. Switalski, Circuit Judge

Honorable Matthew S. Switalski, Circuit Judge

Honorable Joseph Toia, Circuit Judge

Honorable Joseph Toia, Circuit Judge

Honorable Kathryn A. Viviano, Circuit Judge

Honorable Tracey A. Yokich, Circuit Judge

37th District Court (Center Line)

7070 E. Ten Mile Rd.

Center Line, MI 48015

(586) 757-8333

Honorable John M. Chmura, Chief Judge

Honorable Michael Chupa, District Judge

Honorable Suzanne M Faunce, District Judge

Honorable Matthew P. Sabaugh, District Judge

Mr. Robert Curtis, Court Administrator

37th District Court (Warren)

Edward A. Rea Judicial Bldg.

8300 Common Rd.

Warren, MI 48093

(586) 574-4900

Honorable John M. Chmura, Chief Judge

Honorable Michael Chupa, District Judge

Honorable Suzanne M Faunce, District Judge

Honorable Matthew P. Sabaugh, District Judge

Mr. Robert Curtis, Court Administrator

38th District Court (Eastpointe)

16101 Nine Mile Rd.

Eastpointe, MI 48021

(586) 445-5020

Honorable Carl F. Gerds, III, Chief Judge

Ms. Karen Haydett, Court Administrator

39th District Court (Roseville)

29733 Gratiot Ave.

Roseville, MI 48066

(586) 773-2010

Honorable Marco A. Santia, Chief Judge

Honorable Joseph F. Boedeker, District Judge

Honorable Catherine B. Steenland, District Judge

Ms. Melissa M. King, Court Administrator

39th District Court (Fraser)

PO Box 10

City Hall

33000 Garfield Rd.

Fraser, MI 48026

(586) 293-3137

Honorable Marco A. Santia, Chief Judge

Honorable Joseph F. Boedeker, District Judge

Honorable Catherine B. Steenland, District Judge

Ms. Melissa M. King, Court Administrator

40th District Court (St. Clair Shores)

27701 Jefferson Ave.

St. Clair Shores, MI 48081

(586) 445-5280

Honorable Mark A. Fratarcangeli, Chief Judge

Honorable Joseph Craigen Oster, District Judge

Ms. Carolyn A. Povich, Court Administrator

41A District Court (Sterling Heights)

40111 Dodge Park Rd.

Sterling Heights, MI 48313

(586) 446-2500

Honorable Stephen S. Sierawski, Chief Judge

Honorable Michael S. Maceroni, District Judge

Honorable Douglas P. Shepherd, District Judge

Honorable Kimberley Anne Wiegand, District Judge

Mr. Michael Piatek, Court Administrator

41A District Court (Shelby Township)

51660 Van Dyke Ave.

Shelby Township, MI 48316

(586) 739-7325

Honorable Stephen S. Sierawski, Chief Judge

Honorable Michael S. Maceroni, District Judge

Honorable Douglas P. Shepherd, District Judge

Honorable Kimberley Anne Wiegand, District Judge

Ms. Laura Porter, Court Administrator

41B District Court (Clinton Township)

22380 Starks Dr.

Clinton Township, MI 48036

(586) 469-9300

Honorable Carrie Lynn Fuca, Chief Judge

Honorable Linda Davis, District Judge

Honorable Sebastian Lucido, District Judge

42nd District Court (Romeo)

PO Box 6

14713 33 Mile Rd.

Romeo, MI 48065

(586) 752-9679

Honorable James M. Biernat, Jr., Chief Judge

Ms. Julie Bovenschen, Court Administrator

Honorable Denis R. LeDuc, District Judge

Ms. Sandy Kegler, Court Administrator

42nd District Court (New Baltimore)

35071 23 Mile Rd.

New Baltimore, MI 48047

(586) 725-9500

Honorable James M. Biernat, Jr., Chief Judge

Honorable William H. Hackel, III, District Judge

Ms. Marlisa Beauchemin, Court Administrator

WASHTENAW COUNTY

22nd Circuit Court

PO Box 8645

Courthouse

101 E. Huron

Ann Arbor, MI 48107

(734) 222-3270

Honorable David S. Swartz, Chief Judge

Honorable Archie Cameron Brown, Circuit Judge

Honorable Patrick J. Conlin, Jr., Circuit Judge

Honorable Timothy P. Connors, Circuit Judge

Honorable Carol Anne Kuhnke, Circuit Judge

Mr. Daniel Dwyer, Court Administrator

14A-1 District Court (Pittsfield Township)

4133 Washtenaw Ave.

Ann Arbor, MI 48108

(734) 973-4545

Honorable Richard Conlin, District Judge

14A-2 District Court (Ypsilanti)

415 W. Michigan Ave.

Ypsilanti, MI 48197

(734) 484-6690

Honorable Kirk W. Tabbey, District Judge

Mr. Robert Ciolek, Court Administrator

14A-3 District Court (Chelsea)

122 S. Main St.

Chelsea, MI 48118

(734) 475-8606

Honorable Richard Conlin, District Judge

14A-4 District Court (Saline)

1000 N. Maple Rd.

Saline, MI, 48176

(734) 429-2504

Honorable Cedric J. Simpson , District Judge

14B District Court (Ypsilanti Township)

Ypsilanti Township Civic Center

7200 S. Huron River Drive

Ypsilanti, MI 48197

(734) 483-1333

Honorable Charles Pope, Chief Judge

Mr. Mark W. Nelson, Court Administrator

15th District Court (Ann Arbor)

PO Box 8650

Justice Center

301 E. Huron

Ann Arbor, MI 48104

(734) 794-6759

Honorable Joseph F. Burke, Chief Judge

Honorable Elizabeth Pollard Hines, District Judge

Honorable Karen Q. Valvo, District Judge

Ms. Shryl Samborn, Court Administrator

LAPEER COUNTY

40th Circuit Court

Lapeer County Complex

255 Clay Street

Lapeer, MI 48446

(810) 667-0320

Honorable Nick O. Holowka, Chief Judge

Honorable Byron J. Konschuh, Circuit Judge

Ms. Lori Curtiss, Court Administrator

71A District Court (Lapeer)

Lapeer County Complex Building

255 Clay Street

Lapeer, MI 48446

(810) 667-0314

Honorable Nick O. Holowka, Chief Judge

Honorable Laura Cheger Barnard, District Judge

Mr. Gregory K. Wise, Court Administrator

GENESEE COUNTY

7th Circuit Court

Genesee County Courthouse

900 S. Saginaw St.

Flint, MI 48502

(810) 424-4355

Honorable Richard B. Yuille, Chief Judge

Honorable Duncan M. Beagle, Circuit Judge

Honorable Joseph J. Farah, Circuit Judge

Honorable Judith A. Fullerton, Circuit Judge

Honorable John A. Gadola, Circuit Judge

Honorable Archie L. Hayman, Circuit Judge

Honorable Geoffrey L. Neithercut, Circuit Judge

Honorable David J. Newblatt, Circuit Judge

Honorable Michael J. Theile, Circuit Judge

Ms. Barbara A. Menear, Court Administrator

Mr. Sam Olson, Probate Register

67th District Court (Flint)

630 S. Saginaw St.

Flint, MI 48502

(810) 257-3181

Honorable Richard B. Yuille, Chief Judge

Honorable David J. Goggins, District Judge

Mrs. Dena Altheide, Court Administrator

67th District Court (Burton)

4094 Manor Dr.

Burton, MI 48529

(810) 743-5600

Honorable Richard B. Yuille, Chief Judge

Honorable Mark W. Latchana, District Judge

Mrs. Dena Altheide, Court Administrator

67th District Court (Mt. Morris)

11820 N. Saginaw St.

Mt. Morris, MI 48458

(810) 686-7140

Honorable Richard B. Yuille, Chief Judge

Honorable Vikki Bayeh Haley, District Judge

Mrs. Dena Altheide, Court Administrator

67th District Court (Grand Blanc)

8173 S. Saginaw St.

Grand Blanc, MI 48439

(810) 694-2552

Honorable Richard B. Yuille, Chief Judge

Mrs. Dena Altheide, Court Administrator

67th District Court (Flint)

630 S. Saginaw St.

Flint, MI 48502

(810) 766-8968

Honorable Richard B. Yuille, Chief Judge

Honorable William H. Crawford, II, District Judge

Honorable G. David Guinn, District Judge

Mrs. Dena Altheide, Court Administrator

Honorable Herman Marable, Jr., District Judge

Honorable Nathaniel C. Perry, III, District Judge

LIVINGSTON COUNTY

44th Circuit Court

204 S. Highlander Way

Howell, MI 48843

(517) 546-8079

Honorable David Reader, Chief Judge

Honorable Michael P. Hatty, Circuit Judge

Mr. John H. Evans, Court Administrator

53rd District Court (Howell)

204 S. Highlander Way

Howell, MI 48843

(517) 548-1000

Honorable L. Suzanne Geddis, District Judge

Honorable Carol Sue Reader, District Judge

Ms. Francine Zysk, Court Administrator

53rd District Court (Brighton)

224 N 1st St,

Brighton, MI 48116

517-548-1000

Honorable Theresa Brennan, District Judge

KENT COUNTY

17th Circuit Court

Kent County Courthouse

180 Ottawa Ave., NW

Grand Rapids, MI 49503

(616) 632-5220

Honorable Donald A. Johnston, III, Chief Judge

Honorable Paul J. Denenfeld, Circuit Judge

Honorable Kathleen A. Feeney, Circuit Judge

Honorable Dennis B. Leiber, Circuit Judge

Honorable Deborah McNabb, Circuit Judge

Honorable George Jay Quist, Circuit Judge

Honorable J. Joseph Rossi, Circuit Judge

Honorable Paul J. Sullivan, Circuit Judge

Honorable Mark A. Trusock, Circuit Judge

Honorable Christopher P. Yates, Circuit Judge

Honorable Daniel V. Zemaitis, Circuit Judge

Mr. Andrew Thalhammer, Court Administrator

59th District Court (Grandville)

3161 Wilson Ave., S.W.

Grandville, MI 49418

(616) 538-9660

Honorable Peter P. Versluis, Chief Judge

Ms. Julie C. Fend, Court Administrator

59th District Court-Walker

4343 Remembrance Road N.W.

Walker, MI 49534

(616) 453-5765

Honorable Peter P. Versluis, Chief Judge

Ms. Julie C. Fend, Court Administrator

61st District Court (Kent)

Kent County Courthouse

180 Ottawa Ave., NW

Grand Rapids, MI 49503

(616) 632-5700

Honorable Jeanine Nemesi LaVille, Chief Judge

Honorable David J. Buter, District Judge

Honorable Michael J. Distel, District Judge

Honorable Christina Elmore, District Judge

Honorable Jennifer Faber, District Judge

Honorable Kimberly A. Schaefer, District Judge

Mr. Gary Paul Secor, Court Administrator

62A District Court (Wyoming)

Wyoming Justice Center

2650 DeHoop Ave., S.W.

Wyoming, MI 49509

(616) 530-7385

Honorable Steven M. Timmers, Chief Judge

Honorable Pablo Cortes, District Judge

Mr. Christopher Kittmann, Court Administrator

62B District Court (Kentwood)

4740 Walma Ave. SE

Kentwood, MI 49512

(616) 698-9310

Honorable William G. Kelly, Chief Judge

Ms. Michele White, Court Administrator

63rd District Court (Grand Rapids)

1950 E. Beltline Ave. NE

Grand Rapids, MI 49525

(616) 632-7770

Honorable Sara J. Smolenski, Chief Judge

Honorable Jeffrey J. O'Hara, District Judge

Mr. J. Kevin McKay, JD, Court Administrator

INGHAM COUNTY

30th Circuit Court

PO Box 40771

Veterans Memorial Courthouse

313 W. Kalamazoo St.

Lansing, MI 48901

(517) 483-6500

Honorable Janelle A. Lawless, Chief Judge

Honorable Rosemarie E. Aquilina, Circuit Judge

Honorable Laura Baird, Circuit Judge

Honorable Clinton Canady, III, Circuit Judge

Honorable Joyce Draganchuk, Circuit Judge

Honorable James S. Jamo, Circuit Judge

Ms. Shauna Dunnings, Court Administrator

Ingham County Probate Court

Veterans Memorial Courthouse

313 W. Kalamazoo St.

Lansing, MI 48933

(517) 483-6300

Honorable Richard Joseph Garcia, Chief Judge

Honorable R. George Economy, Probate Judge

Mr. George Strander, Court Administrator

Mr. George Strander, Probate Register

54A District Court (Lansing)

City Hall, 6th Floor

124 W. Michigan Ave.

Lansing, MI 48933

(517) 483-4433

Honorable Louise Alderson, Chief Judge

Honorable Patrick F. Cherry, District Judge

Honorable Hugh B. Clarke, Jr., District Judge

Honorable Frank J. DeLuca, District Judge

Ms. Anethia O. Brewer, Court Administrator

54B District Court (East Lansing)

101 Linden St.

East Lansing, MI 48823

(517) 351-7000

Honorable Andrea Andrews Larkin, Chief Judge

Honorable Richard D. Ball, District Judge

Ms. Nicole Evans, Court Administrator

55th District Court (Mason)

700 Buhl Dr.

Mason, MI 48854

(517) 676-8400

Honorable Donald L. Allen, Chief Judge

Honorable Thomas P. Boyd, District Judge

Mr. Michael J. Dillon, Court Administrator

JACKSON COUNTY

4th Circuit Court

312 S. Jackson St.

Jackson, MI 49201

(517) 788-4268

Honorable Thomas D. Wilson, Chief Judge

Mr. Charles M. Adkins, Court Administrator

Honorable Susan Beebe Jordan, Circuit Judge

Honorable Richard N. LaFlamme, Circuit Judge

Honorable John G. McBain, Jr., Circuit Judge

Jackson County Probate Court

Jackson County Courthouse

312 S. Jackson St.

Jackson, MI 49201

(517) 788-4290

Honorable Thomas D. Wilson, Chief Judge

Ms. Julie Kelley, Probate Register

Honorable Diane M. Rappleye, Probate Judge

12th District Court (Jackson)

Jackson County Courthouse

312 S. Jackson St.

Jackson, MI 49201

(517) 788-4260

Honorable Michael J. Klaeren, Chief Judge

Honorable Joseph S. Filip, District Judge

Honorable Daniel A. Goostrey, District Judge

Honorable R. Darryl Mazur, District Judge

Ms. Tamara J. Bates, Court Administrator

LENAWEE COUNTY

39th Circuit Court

Rex B Martin Judicial Building

425 N. Main Street

Adrian, MI 49221

(517) 264-4597

Honorable Margaret Murray-Scholz Noe, Chief Judge

Honorable Anna Marie Anzalone, Circuit Judge

Mrs. Kristi Drake, Court Administrator

Lenawee County Probate Court

Rex B Martin Judicial Building

425 N. Main Street

Adrian, MI 49221

(517) 264-4614

Honorable Margaret Murray-Scholz Noe, Chief Judge

Honorable Gregg P. Iddings, Probate Judge

Ms. Heidi Ross, Probate Register

Mr. John Drahuschak, Court Administrator

2A District Court (Adrian)

Rex B Martin Judicial Bldg

425 N. Main Street

Adrian, MI 49221

(517) 264-4673

Honorable Margaret Murray-Scholz Noe, Chief Judge

Honorable Jonathan L. Poer, District Judge

Honorable Laura J. Schaedler, District Judge

Mr. Mark Fetzer, Court Administrator

MONROE COUNTY

38th Circuit Court

Monroe County Courthouse

106 E. First St.

Monroe, MI 48161

(734) 240-7020

Honorable Jack Vitale, Chief Judge

Honorable Mark S. Braunlich, Circuit Judge

Honorable Michael A. Weipert, Circuit Judge

Honorable Daniel White, Circuit Judge

Ms. Dawn M. Widman, Court Administrator

1st District Court (Monroe)

106 E. First St.

Monroe, MI 48161

(734) 240-7075

Honorable Jack Vitale, Chief Judge

Honorable Terrence P. Bronson, District Judge

Honorable Jarod M. Calkins, District Judge

Ms. Michelle M. Marcero, Court Administrator

ALCONA COUNTY

23rd Circuit Court - Alcona (C23~1)

Alcona County Courthouse

106 5th Street

Harrisville, MI 48740

(989) 724-9400

Honorable Richard E. Vollbach, Jr., Chief Judge

Ms. Alysa Pichler, Court Administrator

Honorable David C. Riffel, Circuit Judge

81st District Court - Alcona (D81~1)

PO Box 385

214 W. Main

Harrisville, MI 48740

(989) 724-9500

Honorable Richard E. Vollbach, Jr., Chief Judge

Honorable Laura A. Frawley, Probate/District Judge

Ms. Alysa Pichler, Court Administrator

ALGER COUNTY

11th Circuit Court - Alger (C11~1)

Alger County

101 Court St.

Munising, MI 49862

(906) 387-2076

Honorable William W. Carmody, Chief Judge

Ms. Jodi Tiglas, Court Administrator

93rd District Court - Alger (D93~1)

Alger County Building

101 Court Street

Munising, MI 49862

(906) 387-3879

Honorable William W. Carmody, Chief Judge

Honorable Mark E. Luoma, District Judge

Ms. Lynne M. Maki, Court Administrator

ALLEGAN COUNTY

48th Circuit Court (C48)

Allegan County Building

113 Chestnut St.

Allegan, MI 49010

(269) 673-0300

Honorable Margaret Bakker, Chief Judge

Honorable Kevin W. Cronin, Circuit Judge

Mr. Michael J. Day, Court Administrator

57th District Court (D57)

Allegan County Building

113 Chestnut St.

Allegan, MI 49010

(269) 673-0400

Honorable William A. Baillargeon, Chief Judge

Ms. Linda Lenahan, Court Administrator

Honorable Joseph S. Skocelas, District Judge

ALPENA COUNTY

26th Circuit Court - Alpena (C26~1)

Alpena County Courthouse

720 W. Chisholm St.

Alpena, MI 49707

(989) 354-9573

Honorable Michael G. Mack, Chief Judge

Ms. Marcia A. Burns, Court Administrator

88th District Court - Alpena (D88~1)

Alpena County Office Building

719 Chisholm St.

Alpena, MI 49707

(989) 354-9678

Honorable Michael G. Mack, Chief Judge

Honorable Thomas J. LaCross, Probate/District Judge

Ms. Mary Margaret Muszynski, Court Administrator

ANTRIM COUNTY

13th Circuit Court - Antrim (C13~1)

PO Box 520

Antrim County Courthouse

205 Cayuga

Bellaire, MI 49615

(231) 533-6353

Honorable Thomas G. Power, Chief Judge

Honorable Kevin Elsenheimer, Circuit Judge

Ms. Teri Quinn, Court Administrator

86th District Court - Antrim (D86~1)

PO Box 597

Antrim County Building

205 Cayuga

Bellaire, MI 49615

(231) 533-6441

Honorable Michael Stepka, Chief Judge

Honorable Thomas J. Phillips, District Judge

Ms. Carol Stocking, Court Administrator

ARENAC COUNTY

23rd Circuit Court - Arenac (C23~2)

Arenac County Courthouse

120 N. Grove

Standish, MI 48658

(989) 846-6131

Honorable Richard E. Vollbach, Jr., Chief Judge

Honorable David C. Riffel, Circuit Judge

Ms. Cristy Slocum, Court Administrator

81st District Court - Arenac (D81~2)

PO Box 129

Arenac County Building

129 Grove St.

Standish, MI 48658

(989) 846-9538

Honorable Richard E. Vollbach, Jr., Chief Judge

Ms. Cristy Slocum, Court Administrator

Honorable Richard E. Vollbach, Jr., Probate/District Judge

BARAGA COUNTY

12th Circuit Court - Baraga (C12~1)

Baraga County Courthouse

16 North Third St.

L'Anse, MI 49946

(906) 524-6183

Honorable Charles R. Goodman, Chief Judge

Ms. Diana Ginter, Court Administrator

97th District Court - Baraga (D97~1)

Baraga County Courthouse

16 N. Third

L'Anse, MI 49946

(906) 524-6100

Honorable Charles R. Goodman, Chief Judge

Honorable Timothy S. Brennan, Probate/District Judge

Ms. Cindy Lundy, Court Administrator

Honorable Mark A. Wisti, District Judge

BARRY COUNTY

5th Circuit Court (C05)

Courthouse

220 W. State Street

Hastings, MI 49058

(269) 945-1286

Honorable William M. Doherty, Chief Judge

Honorable Amy McDowell, Circuit Judge

Ms. Ines Straube, Court Administrator

56B District Court (D56B)

Courts and Law Building

202 W. Court St.

Hastings, MI 49058

(269) 945-1404

Honorable William M. Doherty, Chief Judge

Honorable Michael Lee Schipper, District Judge

Ms. Ines Straube, Court Administrator

BAY COUNTY

18th Circuit Court (C18)

1230 Washington Ave.

Bay City, MI 48708

(989) 895-4265

Honorable Dawn A. Klida, Chief Judge

Honorable Harry P. Gill, Circuit Judge

Mr. Kim Brian Mead, Court Administrator

Honorable Joseph K. Sheeran, Circuit Judge

74th District Court (D74)

1230 Washington Ave.

Bay City, MI 48708

(989) 895-4232

Honorable Dawn A. Klida, Chief Judge

Honorable Mark E. Janer, District Judge

Honorable Timothy J. Kelly, District Judge

Mr. Kim Brian Mead, Court Administrator

BENZIE COUNTY

19th Circuit Court - Benzie (C19~1)

PO Box 377

Benzie County

448 Court Place

Beulah, MI 49617

(231) 882-9671

Honorable David A. Thompson, Chief Judge

Ms. Patricia Ann Heins, Court Administrator

85th District Court - Benzie (D85~1)

PO Box 398

Benzie County

448 Court Place

Beulah, MI 49617

(231) 882-0019

Honorable David A. Thompson, Chief Judge

Honorable John D. Mead, Probate/District Judge

Ms. Kimberly Nowak, Court Administrator

BERRIEN COUNTY

2nd Circuit Court (C02)

Berrien County Courthouse

811 Port St.

St. Joseph, MI 49085

Honorable Gary J. Bruce, Chief Judge

Honorable John M. Donahue, Circuit Judge

Honorable Charles T. LaSata, Circuit Judge

Honorable Angela Pasula, Circuit Judge

Honorable Scott Schofield, Circuit Judge

5th District Court (D05)

Berrien County Courthouse

811 Port St.

St. Joseph, MI 49085

Honorable Gary J. Bruce, Chief Judge

Honorable Arthur J. Cotter, District Judge

Honorable Donna B. Howard, District Judge

Honorable Sterling R. Schrock, District Judge

Honorable Dennis M. Wiley, District Judge

BRANCH COUNTY

15th Circuit Court (C15)

Branch County Courthouse

31 Division St.

Coldwater, MI 49036

(517) 279-4304

Honorable Brent R. Weigle, Chief Judge

Mrs. Pamela Gilchrest, Court Administrator

Honorable P. William O'Grady, Circuit Judge

3A District Court (D03A)

Branch County Courthouse

31 Division St.

Coldwater, MI 49036

(517) 279-4308

Honorable Brent R. Weigle, Chief Judge

Mrs. Sarah K. Collins, Court Administrator

CALHOUN COUNTY

37th Circuit Court (C37)

Calhoun County Justice Center

161 E. Michigan Ave.

Battle Creek, MI 49014

Honorable Michael L. Jaconette, Chief Judge

Honorable John A. Hallacy, Circuit Judge

Honorable Tina Yost Johnson, Circuit Judge

Honorable Brian Kirkham, Circuit Judge

Honorable Sarah Soules Lincoln, Circuit Judge

10th District Court (D10)

Calhoun County Justice Center

161 E. Michigan Ave.

Battle Creek, MI 49014

Honorable Michael L. Jaconette, Chief Judge

Honorable Paul K. Beardslee, District Judge

Honorable Samuel I. Durham, Jr., District Judge

Honorable Franklin K. Line, Jr., District Judge

Honorable James D. Norlander, District Judge

CASS COUNTY

43rd Circuit Court (C43)

Law and Courts Building

60296 M-62

Cassopolis, MI 49031

(269) 445-4412

Honorable Susan L. Dobrich, Chief Judge

Ms. Carol M. Bealor, Court Administrator

Honorable Mark A. Herman, Circuit Judge

4th District Court (D04)

Law and Courts Building

60296 M-62

Cassopolis, MI 49031

(269) 445-4424

Honorable Susan L. Dobrich, Chief Judge

Ms. Nancy Brown, Court Administrator

Honorable Stacey A. Rentfrow, District Judge

CHARLEVOIX COUNTY

33rd Circuit Court (C33)

Charlevoix County Building

301 State Street

Charlevoix, MI 49720

(231) 547-7243

Honorable Roy C. Hayes, III, Chief Judge

Ms. Melinda Morgan, Court Administrator

90th District Court - Charlevoix (D90~1)

Charlevoix County Building

301 State St.

Charlevoix, MI 49720

(231) 547-7227

Honorable James N. Erhart, Chief Judge

Mr. H. Dean Viles, Court Administrator

CHEBOYGAN COUNTY

53rd Circuit Court - Cheboygan (C53~1)

PO Box 70

Cheboygan County Building

870 S. Main Street

Cheboygan, MI 49721

(231) 627-8818

Honorable Scott Lee Pavlich, Chief Judge

Ms. Karen Chapman, Court Administrator

89th District Court - Cheboygan (D89~1)

PO Box 70

Cheboygan County Courthouse

870 S. Main

Cheboygan, MI 49721

(231) 627-8809

Honorable Scott Lee Pavlich, Chief Judge

Ms. Jodi Barrette, Court Administrator

Honorable Maria I. Barton, District Judge

CHIPPEWA COUNTY

50th Circuit Court (C50)

Chippewa County Courthouse

319 Court Street

Sault Ste. Marie, MI 49783

(906) 635-6338

Honorable James P. Lambros, Chief Judge

Mrs. Tina M. Ojala, Court Administrator

91st District Court (D91)

Chippewa County, City-County Building

325 Court Street

Sault Ste. Marie, MI 49783

(906) 635-6320

Honorable James P. Lambros, Chief Judge

Honorable Eric Blubaugh, Probate/District Judge

CLARE COUNTY

55th Circuit Court - Clare (C55~1)

Clare County Courthouse

225 W. Main

Harrison, MI 48625

(989) 426-9237

Honorable Joshua M. Farrell, Chief Judge

Honorable Thomas R. Evans, Circuit Judge

Honorable Roy G. Mienk, Circuit Judge

Dr. Karen Moore, Court Administrator

80th District Court - Clare (D80~1)

Clare County Courthouse

225 W. Main St.

Harrison, MI 48625

(989) 539-7173

Honorable Joshua M. Farrell, Chief Judge

Dr. Karen Moore, Court Administrator

CLINTON COUNTY

29th Circuit Court - Clinton (C29~1)

Clinton County Courthouse

100 E. State St.

St. Johns, MI 48879

(989) 224-5130

Honorable Lisa Sullivan, Chief Judge

Mrs. Mary Kay Goerge, Court Administrator

Honorable Michelle M. Rick, Circuit Judge

Honorable Randy L. Tahvonen, Circuit Judge

65A District Court (D65A)

100 E. State Street

St. Johns, MI 48879

(989) 224-5150

Honorable Lisa Sullivan, Chief Judge

Honorable Michael E. Clarizio, District Judge

Mr. Dan Skorich, Court Administrator

CRAWFORD COUNTY

46th Circuit Court - Crawford (C46~1)

Crawford County Courthouse

200 W. Michigan Ave.

Grayling, MI 49738

(989) 348-2841

Honorable George J. Mertz, Chief Judge

Honorable Colin G. Hunter, Circuit Judge

Ms. Julie Ann McDonald, Court Administrator

87C District Court (D87C)

Crawford County Courthouse

200 W. Michigan Ave.

Grayling, MI 49738

(989) 348-2841

Honorable Monte Burmeister, Chief Judge

Honorable Monte Burmeister, Probate/District Judge

Ms. Julie Ann McDonald, Court Administrator

DELTA COUNTY

47th Circuit Court (C47)

Delta County Building

310 Ludington St.

Escanaba, MI 49829

(906) 789-5103

Honorable Steve Parks, Chief Judge

Honorable John B. Economopoulos, Circuit Judge

Ms. Brenda LaCount, Court Administrator

94th District Court (D94)

Delta County

310 Ludington St.

Escanaba, MI 49829

(906) 789-5106

Honorable Steve Parks, Chief Judge

Ms. Emily DeSalvo, Court Administrator

DICKINSON COUNTY

41st Circuit Court - Dickinson (C41~1)

PO Box 609

Dickinson County Courthouse

705 S. Stephenson St.

Iron Mountain, MI 49801

(906) 774-2266

Honorable Mary Brouillette Barglind, Chief Judge

Honorable C. Joseph Schwedler, Chief Judge

Honorable Richard J. Celello, Circuit Judge

Ms. Roxanne Hornik, Court Administrator

95B District Court - Dickinson (D95B~1)

PO Box 609

Dickinson County Courthouse

705 S. Stephenson St.

Iron Mountain, MI 49801

(906) 774-0506

Honorable Christopher S. Ninomiya, Chief Judge

Honorable C. Joseph Schwedler, Chief Judge

EATON COUNTY

56th Circuit Court (C56)

Eaton County Courthouse

1045 Independence Blvd.

Charlotte, MI 48813

(517) 543-7500

Honorable Thomas K. Byerley, Chief Judge

Honorable Janice K. Cunningham, Circuit Judge

Ms. Beryl J. Frenger, Court Administrator

Honorable John Douglas Maurer, Circuit Judge

56A District Court (D56A)

Eaton County Courthouse

1045 Independence Blvd.

Charlotte, MI 48813

(517) 543-7500

Honorable Thomas K. Byerley, Chief Judge

Ms. Beryl J. Frenger, Court Administrator

Honorable Julie O'Neill, District Judge

Honorable Julie H. Reincke, District Judge

EMMET COUNTY

57th Circuit Court (C57)

Emmet County Building

200 Division

Petoskey, MI 49770

(231) 348-1748

Honorable Charles W. Johnson, Chief Judge

Ms. Cheryl Fitzgerald, Court Administrator

90th District Court - Emmet (D90~2)

Emmet County, City-County Bldg.

200 Division Street

Petoskey, MI 49770

(231) 348-1750

Honorable James N. Erhart, Chief Judge

Ms. Lisa M. Smith, Court Administrator

GLADWIN COUNTY

55th Circuit Court - Gladwin (C55~2)

Gladwin County Courthouse

401 W. Cedar Ave.

Gladwin, MI 48624

(989) 426-9237

Honorable Joshua M. Farrell, Chief Judge

Honorable Thomas R. Evans, Circuit Judge

Honorable Roy G. Mienk, Circuit Judge

Dr. Karen Moore, Court Administrator

80th District Court - Gladwin (D80~2)

Gladwin County Building

401 W. Cedar

Gladwin, MI 48624

(989) 426-9207

Honorable Joshua M. Farrell, Chief Judge

Dr. Karen Moore, Court Administrator

GOGEBIC COUNTY

32nd Circuit Court - Gogebic (C32~1)

Gogebic County Courthouse

200 N. Moore St.

Bessemer, MI 49911

(906) 663-4211

Honorable Joel L. Massie, Chief Judge

Ms. Susan Mitchem, Court Administrator

Honorable Michael Pope, Circuit Judge

98th District Court - Gogebic (D98~1)

Gogebic County Courthouse

200 N. Moore St.

Bessemer, MI 49911

(906) 663-4611

Honorable Joel L. Massie, Chief Judge

Ms. Mary Ahnen, Court Administrator

Honorable Joel L. Massie, Probate/District Judge

GRAND TRAVERSE COUNTY

13th Circuit Court - Grand Traverse (C13~2)

Grand Traverse County Courthouse

328 Washington St.

Traverse City, MI 49684

(231) 922-4701

Honorable Thomas G. Power, Chief Judge

Honorable Kevin Elsenheimer, Circuit Judge

Ms. Teri Quinn, Court Administrator

86th District Court - Grand Traverse (D86~2)

Robert P. Griffin Hall of Justice

280 Washington St.

Traverse City, MI 49684

(231) 922-4580

Honorable Michael Stepka, Chief Judge

Honorable Thomas J. Phillips, District Judge

Ms. Carol Stocking, Court Administrator

HILLSDALE COUNTY

1st Circuit Court (C01)

Courthouse

29 N. Howell

Hillsdale, MI 49242

(517) 437-4321

Honorable Michael R. Smith, Chief Judge

Ms. Cindy Webb, Court Administrator

2B District Court (D02B)

49 N. Howell

Hillsdale, MI 49242

(517) 437-7329

Honorable Michael R. Smith, Chief Judge

Honorable Sara S. Lisznyai, District Judge

Ms. Kris Shaneour, Court Administrator

HOUGHTON COUNTY

12th Circuit Court - Houghton (C12~2)

Houghton County Courthouse

401 E. Houghton Ave.

Houghton, MI 49931

(906) 482-5420

Honorable Charles R. Goodman, Chief Judge

Ms. Diana Ginter, Court Administrator

97th District Court - Houghton (D97~2)

Houghton County Courthouse

401 E. Houghton St.

Houghton, MI 49931

(906) 482-4980

Honorable Charles R. Goodman, Chief Judge

Ms. Ginger Sulisz, Court Administrator

Honorable Mark A. Wisti, District Judge

HURON COUNTY

52nd Circuit Court (C52)

Huron County Building

250 E. Huron

Bad Axe, MI 48413

(989) 269-7112

Honorable David B. Herrington, Chief Judge

Mrs. Leah L. Hatch, Court Administrator

Honorable Gerald M. Prill, Circuit Judge

73B District Court (D73B)

Huron County Building

250 E. Huron Ave.

Bad Axe, MI 48413

(989) 269-9987

Honorable David B. Herrington, Chief Judge

Honorable David L. Clabuesch, Probate/District Judge

Honorable David B. Herrington, Probate/District Judge

Ms. Elaine Moore, Court Administrator

IONIA COUNTY

8th Circuit Court - Ionia (C08~1)

Ionia County Courthouse

100 Main St.

Ionia, MI 48846

(616) 527-5315

Honorable Raymond P. Voet, Chief Judge

Honorable Suzanne Kreeger, Circuit Judge

Honorable Ronald J. Schafer, Circuit Judge

Ms. Tracy L. Szymanski, Court Administrator

Ms. Rachelle Joan Thomas, Court Administrator

64A District Court (D64A)

Ionia County

101 W. Main St.

Ionia, MI 48846

(616) 527-5344

Honorable Raymond P. Voet, Chief Judge

Ms. Cheryl Pinnow, Court Administrator

IOSCO COUNTY

81st District Court - Iosco (D81~3)

PO Box 388

Iosco County Building

422 Lake

Tawas City, MI 48764

(989) 362-4441

Honorable Richard E. Vollbach, Jr., Chief Judge

Ms. Jennifer L. Huebel, Court Administrator

Honorable Christopher P. Martin, Probate/District Judge

81st District Court - Iosco (D81~3)

PO Box 388

Iosco County Building

422 Lake

Tawas City, MI 48764

(989) 362-4441

Honorable Richard E. Vollbach, Jr., Chief Judge

Ms. Jennifer L. Huebel, Court Administrator

Honorable Christopher P. Martin, Probate/District Judge

IRON COUNTY

41st Circuit Court - Iron (C41~2)

Iron County Courthouse

2 S. Sixth St.

Crystal Falls, MI 49920

(906) 875-0659

Honorable Mary Brouillette Barglind, Chief Judge

Honorable C. Joseph Schwedler, Chief Judge

Honorable Richard J. Celello, Circuit Judge

Ms. Lori Ann Willman, Court Administrator

95B District Court - Iron (D95B~2)

Iron County Courthouse

2 S. Sixth Street

Crystal Falls, MI 49920

(906) 875-0659

Honorable Christopher S. Ninomiya, Chief Judge

Honorable C. Joseph Schwedler, Chief Judge

Honorable C. Joseph Schwedler, Probate/District Judge

Ms. Lori Ann Willman, Court Administrator

ISABELLA COUNTY

21st Circuit Court (C21)

Isabella County Courthouse

300 N. Main St.

Mt. Pleasant, MI 48858

(989) 772-0911

Honorable Paul H. Chamberlain, Chief Judge

Ms. Kerri Curtiss, Court Administrator

Honorable Mark H. Duthie, Circuit Judge

76th District Court (D76)

300 N. Main St.

Mt. Pleasant, MI 48858

(989) 772-0911

Honorable Paul H. Chamberlain, Chief Judge

Ms. Kerri Curtiss, Court Administrator

Honorable Eric Janes, District Judge

KALAMAZOO COUNTY

9th Circuit Court (C09)

Kalamazoo County Courthouse

227 W. Michigan Ave.

Kalamazoo, MI 49007

(269) 383-8950

Honorable Curtis J. Bell, Chief Judge

Honorable Paul J. Bridenstine, Circuit Judge

Mr. Thom Canny, Court Administrator

Honorable Gary C. Giguere, Jr., Circuit Judge

Honorable Stephen D. Gorsalitz, Circuit Judge

Mr. Chad Kewish, Court Administrator

Honorable Pamela L. Lightvoet, Circuit Judge

Honorable Alexander C. Lipsey, Circuit Judge

8th District Court (D08)

North Location

227 W. Michigan Ave.

Kalamazoo, MI 49007

(269) 384-8171

Honorable Richard A. Santoni, Chief Judge

Honorable Anne E. Blatchford, District Judge

Ms. Ann Filkins, Court Administrator

Honorable Christopher Haenicke, District Judge

Honorable Julie K. Phillips, District Judge

Honorable Vincent C. Westra, District Judge

KENEENAW COUNTY

12th Circuit Court - Keweenaw (C12~3)

Keweenaw County Courthouse

5095 Fourth Street

Eagle River, MI 49950

(906) 337-2229

Honorable Charles R. Goodman, Chief Judge

Ms. Diana Ginter, Court Administrator

97th District Court - Keweenaw (D97~3)

Keweenaw County Courthouse

5095 Fourth Street

Eagle River, MI 49950

(906) 337-2229

Honorable Charles R. Goodman, Chief Judge

Ms. Roxanne Billing, Court Administrator

Honorable Mark A. Wisti, District Judge

KALKASKA COUNTY

46th Circuit Court - Kalkaska (C46~2)

PO Box 10

Kalkaska County Courthouse

605 N. Birch

Kalkaska, MI 49646

(231) 258-3330

Honorable George J. Mertz, Chief Judge

Ms. Teresa Hill, Court Administrator

Honorable Colin G. Hunter, Circuit Judge

87B District Court (D87B)

PO Box 780

Kalkaska County Governmental Center

605 N. Birch Street

Kalkaska, MI 49646

(231) 258-9031

Honorable Lynne Marie Buday, Chief Judge

Honorable Lynne Marie Buday, Probate/District Judge

Ms. Teresa Hill, Court Administrator

LAKE COUNTY

51st Circuit Court - Lake (C51~1)

Lake County

800 Tenth Street

Baldwin, MI 49304

(231) 745-4614

Honorable Peter J. Wadel, Chief Judge

Honorable Mark S. Wickens, Chief Judge

Mr. Jeffrey A. Nadig, Court Administrator

Honorable Susan K. Sniegowski, Circuit Judge

79th District Court - Lake (D79~1)

Lake County

800 10th Street

Baldwin, MI 49304

(231) 745-4614

Honorable Peter J. Wadel, Chief Judge

Honorable Mark S. Wickens, Chief Judge

Mr. Jeffrey A. Nadig, Court Administrator

Honorable Mark S. Wickens, Probate/District Judge

LEELANAU COUNTY

13th Circuit Court - Leelanau (C13~3)

8527 E. Government Center Dr.

Suttons Bay, MI 49682

(231) 256-9803

Honorable Thomas G. Power, Chief Judge

Honorable Kevin Elsenheimer, Circuit Judge

Ms. Teri Quinn, Court Administrator

86th District Court - Leelanau (D86~3)

8527 E. Government Center Dr.

Suttons Bay, MI 49682

(231) 256-8250

Honorable Michael Stepka, Chief Judge

Honorable Thomas J. Phillips, District Judge

Ms. Carol Stocking, Court Administrator

LUCE COUNTY

11th Circuit Court - Luce (C11~2)

Luce County Government Building

407 W. Harrie

Newberry, MI 49868

(906) 293-5521

Honorable William W. Carmody, Chief Judge

Ms. Jodi Tiglas, Court Administrator

92nd District Court - Luce (D92~1)

Luce County

407 W. Harrie St.

Newberry, MI 49868

(906) 293-5531

Honorable William W. Carmody, Chief Judge

Ms. Jeanine Blakely, Court Administrator

Honorable Beth Gibson, District Judge

MACKINAC COUNTY

11th Circuit Court - Mackinac (C11~3)

Mackinac County Courthouse

100 Marley St.

St. Ignace, MI 49781

(906) 643-7300

Honorable William W. Carmody, Chief Judge

Ms. Jodi Tiglas, Court Administrator

92nd District Court - Mackinac (D92~2)

Mackinac County Courthouse

100 Marley St.

St. Ignace, MI 49781

(906) 643-7321

Honorable William W. Carmody, Chief Judge

Ms. Jeanine Blakely, Court Administrator

Honorable Beth Gibson, District Judge

MANISTEE COUNTY

19th Circuit Court - Manistee (C19~2)

Manistee County

415 3rd Street

Manistee, MI 49660

(231) 723-6664

Honorable David A. Thompson, Chief Judge

Ms. Patricia Ann Heins, Court Administrator

85th District Court - Manistee (D85~2)

Manistee County Courthouse

415 Third St.

Manistee, MI 49660

(231) 723-5010

Honorable David A. Thompson, Chief Judge

Honorable Thomas N. Brunner, Probate/District Judge

Mr. Jared C. Henry, Court Administrator

MARQUETTE COUNTY

25th Circuit Court (C25)

Courthouse

234 W. Baraga

Marquette, MI 49855

(906) 225-8205

Honorable Jennifer Mazzuchi, Chief Judge

Ms. Charity Mason, Court Administrator

96th District Court (D96)

Marquette County Courthouse

234 W. Baraga Ave.

Marquette, MI 49855

(906) 225-8235

Honorable Roger W. Kangas, Chief Judge

Ms. Charity Mason, Court Administrator

Honorable Karl Weber, District Judge

MASON COUNTY

51st Circuit Court - Mason (C51~2)

Mason County Courthouse

304 E. Ludington Ave.

Ludington, MI 49431

(231) 845-0516

Honorable Peter J. Wadel, Chief Judge

Honorable Mark S. Wickens, Chief Judge

Ms. Denise Meissner, Court Administrator

Honorable Susan K. Sniegowski, Circuit Judge

79th District Court - Mason (D79~2)

Mason County Courthouse

304 E. Ludington Avenue

Ludington, MI 49431

(231) 843-4130

Honorable Peter J. Wadel, Chief Judge

Honorable Mark S. Wickens, Chief Judge

Ms. Patricia Baker, Court Administrator

MECOSTA COUNTY

49th Circuit Court - Mecosta (C49~1)

Mecosta County Courthouse

400 Elm Street

Big Rapids, MI 49307

(231) 592-0780

Honorable Scott P. Hill-Kennedy, Chief Judge

Honorable Kimberly L. Booher, Circuit Judge

Ms. Terri L. Pontz, Court Administrator

77th District Court - Mecosta (D77~1)

Mecosta County Building

400 Elm Street

Big Rapids, MI 49307

(231) 592-0799

Honorable Scott P. Hill-Kennedy, Chief Judge

Honorable Peter Jaklevic, District Judge

Mr. Thomas Lyons, Court Administrator

MENOMINEE COUNTY

41st Circuit Court - Menominee (C41~3)

Menominee County Courthouse

839 10th Ave.

Menominee, MI 49858

(906) 863-8981

Honorable Mary Brouillette Barglind, Chief Judge

Honorable C. Joseph Schwedler, Chief Judge

Honorable Richard J. Celello, Circuit Judge

95A District Court (D95A)

Menominee County Courthouse

839 10th Ave.

Menominee, MI 49858

(906) 863-8532

Honorable Jeffrey G. Barstow, Chief Judge

Ms. Linda Menacher, Court Administrator

MIDLAND COUNTY

42nd Circuit Court (C42)

Midland County Courthouse

301 W. Main Street

Midland, MI 48640

(989) 832-6657

Honorable Stephen Carras, Chief Judge

Honorable Michael J. Beale, Circuit Judge

Mr. Lance Dexter, Court Administrator

75th District Court (D75)

Midland County Courthouse

301 W. Main Street

Midland, MI 48640

(989) 832-6709

Honorable Stephen Carras, Chief Judge

Honorable Michael Carpenter, District Judge

Mr. Lance Dexter, Court Administrator

Mr. Gerald Ladwig, Court Administrator

MISSAUKEE COUNTY

28th Circuit Court - Missaukee (C28~1)

PO Box 800

Missaukee County Courthouse

111 S. Canal St.

Lake City, MI 49651

(231) 839-4967

Honorable William M. Fagerman, Chief Judge

Ms. Flora Grundy, Court Administrator

84th District Court - Missaukee (D84~1)

PO Box 800

Missaukee County Courthouse

111 S. Canal St.

Lake City, MI 49651

(231) 839-4590

Honorable William M. Fagerman, Chief Judge

Ms. Carol Palmer, Court Administrator

Honorable Charles R. Parsons, Probate/District Judge

Honorable Audrey D. Van Alst, District Judge

MONTMORENCY COUNTY

26th Circuit Court - Montmorency (C26~2)

PO Box 789

Montmorency County Courthouse

M 32

Atlanta, MI 49709

(989) 785-8022

Honorable Michael G. Mack, Chief Judge

Ms. Marcia A. Burns, Court Administrator

88th District Court - Montmorency (D88~2)

PO Box 789

Montmorency County Courthouse

Atlanta, MI 49709

(989) 785-8035

Honorable Michael G. Mack, Chief Judge

Honorable Benjamin T. Bolser, Probate/District Judge

Ms. Kristen Cheedie, Court Administrator

MONTCALM COUNTY

8th Circuit Court - Montcalm (C08~2)

PO Box 296

Montcalm County Courthouse

631 N. State Street

Stanton, MI 48888

(989) 831-7363

Honorable Raymond P. Voet, Chief Judge

Honorable Suzanne Kreeger, Circuit Judge

Honorable Ronald J. Schafer, Circuit Judge

Ms. Tracy L. Szymanski, Court Administrator

Ms. Rachelle Joan Thomas, Court Administrator

64B District Court (D64B)

Montcalm County

617 N. State

Stanton, MI 48888

(989) 831-7450

Honorable Raymond P. Voet, Chief Judge

Honorable Donald R. Hemingsen, District Judge

Ms. Janet Lyndrup, Court Administrator

NEWAYGO COUNTY

27th Circuit Court - Newaygo (C27~1)

PO Box 885

Newaygo County Courthouse

1092 Newell

White Cloud, MI 49349

(231) 689-7269

Honorable H. Kevin Drake, Chief Judge

Ms. Wendy Jarvis, Court Administrator

Honorable Robert D. Springstead, Circuit Judge

78th District Court - Newaygo (D78~1)

PO Box 129

Newaygo County Courthouse

1092 Newell

White Cloud, MI 49349

(231) 689-7257

Honorable H. Kevin Drake, Chief Judge

Ms. Wendy Jarvis, Court Administrator

Ms. Diane M. Reinke, Court Administrator

14th Circuit Court (C14)

Michael E. Kobza Hall of Justice

990 Terrace

Muskegon, MI 49442

(231) 724-6251

Honorable William C. Marietti, Chief Judge

Honorable Timothy G. Hicks, Circuit Judge

Honorable Kathy L. Hoogstra, Circuit Judge

Honorable Annette Rose Smedley, Circuit Judge

Ms. Sandra M. Vanderhyde, Court Administrator

60th District Court (D60)

Michael E. Kobza Hall of Justice

990 Terrace St.

Muskegon, MI 49442

(231) 724-6283

Honorable Raymond J. Kostrzewa, Jr., Chief Judge

Honorable Harold F. Closz, III, District Judge

Mr. Patrick A. Finnegan, Court Administrator

Honorable Maria Ladas Hoopes, District Judge

Honorable Geoffrey Thomas Nolan, District Judge

OCEANA COUNTY

27th Circuit Court - Oceana (C27~2)

Oceana County Building

100 S. State Street

Hart, MI 49420

(231) 873-3977

Honorable H. Kevin Drake, Chief Judge

Ms. Tonya Selig, Court Administrator

Honorable Robert D. Springstead, Circuit Judge

78th District Court - Oceana (D78~2)

PO Box 471

Oceana County Building

100 State Street

Hart, MI 49420

(231) 873-4530

Honorable H. Kevin Drake, Chief Judge

Ms. Jo A. Gowell, Court Administrator

OGEMAW COUNTY

34th Circuit Court - Ogemaw (C34~1)

Ogemaw County Building

806 W. Houghton Ave.

West Branch, MI 48661

(989) 275-7610

Honorable Richard E. Noble, Chief Judge

Honorable Robert Bennett, Circuit Judge

Ms. Terri Collini, Court Administrator

82nd District Court - Ogemaw (D82~1)

PO Box 365

Ogemaw County Building

806 W. Houghton Ave.

West Branch, MI 48661

(989) 345-5040

Honorable Richard E. Noble, Chief Judge

Ms. Diane Rau, Court Administrator

ONTOAGON COUNTY

32nd Circuit Court - Ontonagon (C32~2)

Ontonagon County Courthouse

725 Greenland Rd.

Ontonagon, MI 49953

(906) 884-4699

Honorable Joel L. Massie, Chief Judge

Ms. Susan Mitchem, Court Administrator

Honorable Michael Pope, Circuit Judge

98th District Court - Ontonagon (D98~2)

Ontonagon County

725 Greenland Rd.

Ontonagon, MI 49953

(906) 884-2865

Honorable Joel L. Massie, Chief Judge

Honorable Janis M. Burgess, Probate/District Judge

Ms. Mary Jane Loukus, Court Administrator

OSCEOLA COUNTY

49th Circuit Court - Osceola (C49~2)

Osceola County Courthouse

301 W. Upton

Reed City, MI 49677

(231) 832-3261

Honorable Scott P. Hill-Kennedy, Chief Judge

Honorable Kimberly L. Booher, Circuit Judge

Ms. Terri L. Pontz, Court Administrator

77th District Court - Osceola (D77~2)

Osceola County Courthouse Annex

410 W. Upton

Reed City, MI 49677

(231) 832-6155

Honorable Scott P. Hill-Kennedy, Chief Judge

Mr. Daniel Edward Clise, Sr., Court Administrator

Honorable Peter Jaklevic, District Judge

46th Circuit Court - Otsego (C46~3)

800 Livingston Blvd.

Gaylord, MI 49735

(989) 731-7500

Honorable George J. Mertz, Chief Judge

Ms. Victoria A. Courterier, Court Administrator

Honorable Colin G. Hunter, Circuit Judge

87A District Court (D87A)

Otsego County, Alpine Center

800 Livingston Blvd.

Gaylord, MI 49735

(989) 731-0201

Honorable Michael K. Cooper, Chief Judge

Honorable Michael K. Cooper, Probate/District Judge

Ms. Victoria A. Courterier, Court Administrator

PRESQUE ISLE COUNTY

53rd Circuit Court - Presque Isle (C53~2)

PO Box 110

Presque Isle County

151 E. Huron

Rogers City, MI 49779

(989) 734-3288

Honorable Scott Lee Pavlich, Chief Judge

Ms. Karen Chapman, Court Administrator

89th District Court - Presque Isle (D89~2)

PO Box 110

Presque Isle County Building

151 E. Huron

Rogers City, MI 49779

(989) 734-2411

Honorable Scott Lee Pavlich, Chief Judge

Honorable Maria I. Barton, District Judge

Ms. Kristy Hardies, Court Administrator

Honorable Donald J. McLennan, Probate/District Judge

ROSCOMMON COUNTY

34th Circuit Court - Roscommon (C34~2)

PO Box 818

Roscommon County Courthouse

500 Lake Street

Roscommon, MI 48653

(989) 275-7610

Honorable Richard E. Noble, Chief Judge

Honorable Robert Bennett, Circuit Judge

Ms. Terri Collini, Court Administrator

82nd District Court - Roscommon (D82~2)

Roscommon County Building

500 Lake St.

Roscommon, MI 48653

(989) 275-5312

Honorable Richard E. Noble, Chief Judge

Ms. Donna Lowe, Court Administrator

ST CLAIR COUNTY COUNTY

31st Circuit Court (C31)

County Building

201 McMorran Blvd.

Port Huron, MI 48060

(810) 985-2031

Honorable Daniel J. Kelly, Chief Judge

Honorable Cynthia A. Lane, Circuit Judge

Honorable Michael L. West, Circuit Judge

72nd District Court (D72)

201 McMorran Blvd.

Port Huron, MI 48060

(810) 985-2072

Honorable Daniel J. Kelly, Chief Judge

Mr. Brian Matthew Henderson, Court Administrator

Honorable Michael L. Hulewicz, District Judge

Honorable John D. Monaghan, District Judge

Honorable Cynthia Siemen Platzer, District Judge

SAGINAW COUNTY

10th Circuit Court (C10)

111 S. Michigan Ave.

Saginaw, MI 48602

(989) 790-5470

Honorable Terry L. Clark, Chief Judge

Honorable Janet M. Boes, Circuit Judge

Honorable James T. Borchard, Circuit Judge

Honorable Andre' R. Borrello, Circuit Judge

Honorable Darnell Jackson, Circuit Judge

Honorable Robert L. Kaczmarek, Circuit Judge

Ms. Paula J. McGlown, Court Administrator

70th District Court - Division 1 (D70-1)

111 S. Michigan Ave.

Saginaw, MI 48602

(989) 790-5363

Honorable Terry L. Clark, Chief Judge

Ms. Linda James, Court Administrator

Honorable M. Randall Jurrens, District Judge

70th District Court - Division 2 (D70-2)

111 S. Michigan Ave.

Saginaw, MI 48602

(989) 790-5363

Honorable Terry L. Clark, Chief Judge

Honorable Alfred T. Frank, District Judge

Honorable David D. Hoffman, District Judge

Ms. Linda James, Court Administrator

Honorable Manvel Trice, III, District Judge

ST JOSEPH COUNTY

45th Circuit Court (C45)

PO Box 189

St. Joseph County Courthouse

125 W. Main

Centreville, MI 49032

(269) 467-5500

Honorable Jeffrey C. Middleton, Chief Judge

Ms. Kathryn Sue Griffin, Court Administrator

Honorable Paul E. Stutesman, Circuit Judge

3B District Court (D03B)

PO Box 67

Courthouse

125 W. Main

Centreville, MI 49032

(269) 467-5500

Honorable Jeffrey C. Middleton, Chief Judge

Honorable Robert Pattison, District Judge

Ms. Tabitha Wedge, Court Administrator

ST CLAIR COUNTY COUNTY

31st Circuit Court (C31)

County Building

201 McMorran Blvd.

Port Huron, MI 48060

(810) 985-2031

Honorable Daniel J. Kelly, Chief Judge

Honorable Cynthia A. Lane, Circuit Judge

Honorable Michael L. West, Circuit Judge

72nd District Court (D72)

201 McMorran Blvd.

Port Huron, MI 48060

(810) 985-2072

Honorable Daniel J. Kelly, Chief Judge

Mr. Brian Matthew Henderson, Court Administrator

Honorable Michael L. Hulewicz, District Judge

Honorable John D. Monaghan, District Judge

Honorable Cynthia Siemen Platzer, District Judge

SANILAC COUNTY

24th Circuit Court (C24)

Sanilac County Courthouse

60 W. Sanilac

Sandusky, MI 48471

(810) 648-2120

Honorable Donald A. Teeple, Chief Judge

Ms. Christina Baldwin, Court Administrator

73A District Court (D73A)

Sanilac County Courthouse

60 West Sanilac Avenue

Sandusky, MI 48471

(810) 648-3250

Honorable Donald A. Teeple, Chief Judge

Ms. Traci Franzel, Court Administrator

Honorable Gregory S. Ross, Probate/District Judge

SCHOOLCRAFT COUNTY

11th Circuit Court - Schoolcraft (C11~4)

PO Box 186

Schoolcraft County Courthouse

300 Walnut

Manistique, MI 49854

(906) 341-3655

Honorable William W. Carmody, Chief Judge

Ms. Jodi Tiglas, Court Administrator

93rd District Court - Schoolcraft (D93~2)

Schoolcraft County Courthouse

300 Walnut St.

Manistique, MI 49854

(906) 341-3630

Honorable William W. Carmody, Chief Judge

Honorable Mark E. Luoma, District Judge

Mr. David Maddox, Court Administrator

TUSCOLA COUNTY

54th Circuit Court (C54)

Tuscola County Courthouse

440 N. State St.

Caro, MI 48723

(989) 673-3330

Honorable Amy Grace Gierhart, Chief Judge

Ms. Caryn Marie Michalak, Court Administrator

71B District Court (D71B)

Tuscola County Courthouse

440 N. State St.

Caro, MI 48723

(989) 672-3800

Honorable Amy Grace Gierhart, Chief Judge

Honorable Kim David Glaspie, District Judge

Ms. Sheila Long, Court Administrator

SHIAWASSEE COUNTY

35th Circuit Court (C35)

208 N. Shiawassee St.

Corunna, MI 48817

(989) 743-2239

Honorable Ward L. Clarkson, Chief Judge

Ms. Krissi Lab, Court Administrator

Honorable Matthew J. Stewart, Circuit Judge

66th District Court (D66)

Shiawassee County Courts Building

110 E. Mack St.

Corunna, MI 48817

(989) 743-2395

Honorable Ward L. Clarkson, Chief Judge

Mr. Dale A. DeGarmo, Court Administrator

Honorable Terrance P. Dignan, District Judge

VAN BUREN COUNTY

36th Circuit Court (C36)

Van Buren County Courthouse

212 Paw Paw St.

Paw Paw, MI 49079

(269) 657-8218

Honorable Kathleen Brickley, Chief Judge

Honorable Jeffrey J. Dufon, Circuit Judge

Mr. E. Frank Hardester, Court Administrator

7th District Court (D07)

Courthouse

212 Paw Paw St.

Paw Paw, MI 49079

(269) 657-8222

Honorable Kathleen Brickley, Chief Judge

Mr. James R. Becker, Court Administrator

Honorable Arthur H. Clarke, III, District Judge

Mr. E. Frank Hardester, Court Administrator

Mr. Craig Hess, Court Administrator

Honorable Michael T. McKay, District Judge

WEXFORD COUNTY

28th Circuit Court - Wexford (C28~2)

Wexford County Courthouse

437 E. Division

Cadillac, MI 49601

(231) 779-9490

Honorable William M. Fagerman, Chief Judge

Ms. Flora Grundy, Court Administrator

84th District Court - Wexford (D84~2)

Wexford County Courthouse

437 E. Division St.

Cadillac, MI 49601

(231) 779-9515

Honorable William M. Fagerman, Chief Judge

Ms. Kelly Dostal, Court Administrator

Honorable Audrey D. Van Alst, District Judge

www.ingramcontent.com/pod-product-compliance
Lightning Source LLC
Chambersburg PA
CBHW071855200326
41519CB00016B/4399